By Christopher Dow

Fiction
Effigy
> Book I: Stroud
> Book II: Oakdale

The Books of Bob
> Devil of a Time
> Jumping Jehovah

The Clay Guthrie Mysteries
> The Dead Detective
> Landscape with Beast
> The Texas Troll Unlimited
> Darkness Insatable

Roadkill
The Werewolf and Tide, and Other Compulsions

Nonfiction
Lord of the Loincloth (nonfiction novel)
Book of Curiosities: Adventures in the Paranormal
Occasional Pilgrimage: Essays on Film, Literature, and Other Matters
Living the Story: The Meandering, True, and Sometimes Strange
> Adventures of an Unknown Writer, Vols. I & II

Poetry
City of Dreams
The Trip Out
Texas White Line Fever
Networks
A Dilapidation of Machinery
Puzzle Pieces: Selected Poems

Art
Harboring with Arabesques: The Art of Christopher Dow

Martial Arts
The Wellspring: An Inquiry into the Nature of Chi
Circling the Square: Observations on the Dynamics of Tai Chi Chuan
Elements of Power: Essays on the Art and Practice of Tai Chi Chuan
Alchemy of Breath: An Introduction to Chi Kung
Leaves on the Wind: A Survey of Martial Arts Literature, Vols. I–VI

Editor
Drifts: Texas Writers: Interviews and Profiles
The Abby Stone: The Poetry of Bartholo Dias
The Best of Phosphene
The Best of Dialog

NETWORKS

NETWORKS

Christopher Dow

Phosphene Publishing Company
Temple, Texas

Networks
© 2013 by Christopher Dow
ISBN 13: 978-0-9796968-8-6
ISBN 10: 0-9796968-8-7

Published by
Phosphene Publishing Company
Temple, Texas, U.S.A.
phosphenepublishing.com

4.1

For Julie

CONTENTS

NETWORKS

Woman, Horse

Wild horse and woman
And a beginning
That now and ever shall be
Altogether different than its predecessor—
A return that is without sacrifice
And places hymns and gifts
And with deep devotion
Sanctifies the bleeding roses.
And the woman watches over a world eclipsed,
Sees through the sun, and through her offering,
Flies without wings.
How she flies.
How the horse touches her
With secrets, with gems of tears,
With life, the prairie, and miracles.

Welcome to talk too easy to discredit,
Too hasty to convert in its attempt
To tame this lovely horse
With a magic brocade woven
While old, leather-skinned,
Sitting by the door,
Smoking a pipe,
Released in miracle and revelation:

The rider on the pale horse is death,
And the heavens are giving birth,
Touching a soul. And the woman—
Exceptional centaur,
Active, adventurous, experiment
Described in human torso
And healing transformation—
Flies without wings
Through the Way,
Through the power,
Through moderated carnage and rules,
Through the emotional odyssey
Of a challenging and pioneering
Yet familiar grace.

It is the prospect of a journey
With which she is truly filled
As she flies without touch,
And knows whispers and the man who listens.
The symbol and sacred objects
Are as comprehensive as recommendation,
As special as unique need.

Let me tell you about this, the best in my life,
Riding into myth and fable and imagination:
As long as I have sought to be free
Of this age oppressed, perfect, comic, rare,

There have been catalyst, revelation, horse.
Who wouldn't attempt to fathom experiences
Found in each of these islands of confessed love?

Whether you believe or not,
As I stumbled the way home,
Seeking shelter from supernatural gestures
And documentable sources,
The heavens opened, and I beheld a white horse—
Not a yearling but mature and threatening,
Weaving events with the voice of herds—
And upon it, I sped over the world
To destroy the Babylon of interpretation,
Worked for the goddess of that wild devil
To gather the holy pearl of tragedy
From an oyster outraged,
Only to learn that description
Is a country all its own,
Dancing away its destiny to flute music.

Crazy horse. Crazy vision.
Yet the dawn does more than light opinion
Or grab the spirit of connections
Or enchant the nomad heart of things.
Sparks fly free, shatter against the world.
A young star, an ancient moon dance, a healing.

The best prayers make a good man or woman
Infinitely splendid, beautiful, full,
Automatically entered into perilous experience.
And one sneaked into our lives,
Stole distance with a wild and ultimate liberty
Masquerading as darkness and thunder.
And the thunder shared its heart.

Flight, Time, and the Hollow Heart

Riding a wind stream,
The view is wide, the air pure,
And I hoped to catch a glimpse
Of hidden truths dancing mimetic
On a shore beyond the horizon.
But I had the heart of a beast
Seeking the way to the heavens
By tracing the path of a shooting star,
Seeking flowers amid garbage
And the last drop of innocence
In the gossip of hollow men,
Seeking echoes of the shadow within
After they are consumed in flames.

And the wind groaned
Across ancient fantasies of a crumbling id
And took to vagrancy
On unhallowed ground.
It was an occasion of much mischief;
It was a shock;
It was a moment in which
I sank with weariness,
Flight hopeless.

Earthbound, I sought
The location of precious serenity
And the rise of an ancient elegance
As pure and haunting
As caresses insinuating
That beauty can reside in a hollow heart.
But when awe becomes hyperbole
Kidnapped by eager, ambitious shame,
Speech of the heart
Becomes speech of the mouth,
And wayward thought
An alternative to hope.

To fly again, I must know the heart
That holds memories like a mirror
Holds the reversed identity of the unknown
In its silver face
And know with certainty that death
Is a warning to the living
That dead men are forever true.

But the last time I woke,
I seemed to come back from farther away,
And I came to understand
I might never know the secrets.
I have no heart to say more.

Admit it, wind dancer:
Time is up.
Go.

Where Is Pandora's Box?

Pandora's Gifts

Pandora, first woman on Earth.
Ordered by Zeus.
Created by Hephaestus, god of craftsmanship,
Using water and earth.
Named "All the Gifts."
Gift to man
To spoil his happiness,
To punish him for the gift of fire
Bestowed by Prometheus.
All the gods gave her gifts—
Zeus, bearer of mystery and power, the box,
That she might thoroughly bedevil mankind.

Which god gave her the gift of curiosity
Without the gift of caution?
Epimetheus warned Pandora not to open the box,
But apparently no god gave her the gift
Of listening to the gods.
Which god forgot to impart the question:
"Once the box is open, how do you close it?"

Opening

She had to know what was inside.
Innocent, but more and more inquisitive.
Just a peek inside.
Classic, silent, complete, organized.
Picking the lock.
Lifting the forbidden lid.
Just a peek….

A lively curiosity, a mysterious casket,
And a legacy of scourge and disease.
There go monkeypox and other tiny bugs
Jumping from animals to people.
There hop land grabs and uncontrollable
Situations without perspective.
There inch separatism, secession, and irredentism
In the name of nationalism,
Yet responsible for ever-growing fragmentation.
And here slink shadows, secrecy, and moral decay.

The flu virus genome fit in there—
Should the Pandora's box of negotiations
On public health be reopened?
The human testing of toxics
Once took place in a lab there,

But now, chemical substances invade
Our food, air, and water.
A truck packed with explosives
Once used it as a garage.
Fetishes, whips, chains,
And other family entertainments spilled out
Right after the twin sprites
Unaccountability and Anarchy,
The weaponization of the human psyche,
And a lump of legal lies.

And then there were the shoes.
It was Pandora's shoebox:
A cornucopia of ugly, senseless footwear
Designed to torture the feet of Imelda Marcos.

Not surprisingly, other things slithered.

Aftermath

Pandora.
It was a character test.
A first offering.
A new story.

Now it is an old one.
No wonder the myth is widely known,
With boxes like matryoshka dolls
That grow ever larger and more complex:
Cuneiform tablets, scrolls,
Books, radio, television,
The Internet, and virtual reality.
Only now, we are the demons
We unleash upon ourselves.

Where is Pandora's box
Now that the winds of ill have escaped?
It later turned up in the hands of a sorcerer,
Though how he came by it is unknown,
Save that he traced back the ideas
That winged free without
Knowing where they might alight.
Did he look inside to see
The one small waif
Pandora shut back in
Like the crippled boy
Shut out by the Pied Piper?

Loose Ends

There is no point in imagining
A world where Pandora's box
Has remained unopened,
Where sin, evil, and confusion
Have not entered the world,
Where the darkest part
Of the human psyche does not
Dwell in poisons and fog.

And at the very bottom of the box,
After everything else has escaped,
Lies Hope.
Not because it was least
Or sequestered, but because
Pandora's box is our own hearts,
Each like an open sesame
Or a many-layered puzzle,
Each harboring a hope for ourselves
Rarely bestowed upon others,
Often emitting foul radiations.

We can only hope
That the Clown,
In the desperate final act,
Recaptures the tricksters,
Reassembles Pandora's Box,
And saves the world,
Hope at his side.

Speak to Me

1

Speak to me
When you walk in music.
Talk of the unusual and novel and reasonable.
Speak to me
When you move in welcome,
But do not talk of prayer or serenity or faith
If you do not hear the meadowlark sing
Or the whispered music of living echoes
That err, lost and alone.
Do not talk if you have the answer.
Better to say random things
Or to speak of grief, of love,
Of what endures in ordinary hearing,
Of overwhelming reality enclosed in a news clip
Or a pocket.
Pull out the words that say
You will take me anywhere but back.
You must choose the answers
As well as the questions and correct grammar.

2

Do not speak to me in French.
I do not want to translate.
Do not speak to me of 1950.
I do not want to return.
Do not speak to me in self-study.
I do not want anything but the world.

I will send you no magic coins
That lie in the pockets of silent audiences
To purchase permission and despair
Rolling like thunder across the skies—
Thunder that bombards, saturates, overwhelms.
So speak not of the nightmares
Of people who cannot answer
Or ancestors who are past desire,
But promise, and I promise not
To speak to you in a language
Irrelevant and abandoned
By experience, spirituality, and passion.

And if you do not speak to me again,
Let the dance speak as if we are young,
Embracing fears, remembering nothing
But that we have lived long enough
To have stood rooted in shadows of sight

And drift in lagoons whose waters whisper
Of desert shores that know no prophets.
Long enough to have been mad for years.

3

I wish never to investigate
The instinctual need for communication
Only to discover that the species is mute
And that I cannot see clearly into your eyes
Though they look straight into mine.
Failures of language forever wander streets
Where windows are paneless
And doors remain unopened.

If only you would never
Speak like the dead.
If only you would never
Uncover our need to communicate
Only to speak in hesitation.
If only you would falter—
If only for a second,
If only out of resemblance,
If only in whispers of circumstance,
For circumstances become aware,
But intentions become honesty deceived

And locked in a room.
Your silence is a test of wills,
A mechanism of punishment,
A breath that refuses to breathe,
A language that I cannot hear.

4

I could sweat blood,
But I could never follow the flock.
I could believe I earnestly desire to know myself,
But I can't speak about that which can't be found
With facts or surprise or fierce footsteps.
Enjoyment fails me
Because I am in contact
With the fruit and foliage of the gentle dark,
The emotionless face.
Let me hear you turn the pages
Of tormented fears
And ignore ghosts who refuse commands.

5

Sit silently for a moment,
Then merely say
I have entered wrong, finite,
Scoffing at gravity, listening
With evoked guilt and powerlessness,
And not knowing how to reply
To private good deeds.

I would have reached out
And inspired silent anger,
Ignored the facts of anxious experience,
Answered questions of conditional relativity,
And requested hope's secure restrictions
Beyond necessity and welcome,
Except I had a notion and a decision
And nothing to lose
But grace and the gift of dialogue
And summers remembered
And travel along unaccustomed ways.
So, if I panic, speak to me calmly,
For I am in a darkness of illusion
From which I am not yet born.

6

Rock, speak to me,
But speak slowly, speak lowly
Because your strong emotions
Drive me to be alone
And to trouble.
Don't mislead me
Like the calm before a storm.
My heart is swelling;
There is no telling where it starts
Or how it ends.

Is it constructive discharge
Or the swift sweet now
That, tense and slow,
Stops our conversation?
It is my firm belief that I am independent
And can be trusted with tears.
Sooner or later one of us is going to speak
Of indescribable happiness,
Though I cannot predict where, when, or how.
In prison, we must get permission before we speak
Even if we want to speak,
Even if we must speak immediately,
Even if silence means annihilation.

7

I hate the kind of talk that distracts,
That goes but one inch
And takes that inch for a mile,
That doesn't address comfort for the injured
Or the many issues we all must face.
But we are all too busy talking to speak.
Unless I apply the powers of listening,
Nothing will speak to me of consequence,
Of relationships, of the days that surround me
With pure emotion and visceral adventure.
Though malice is ever-vigilant and lurking,
Extravagance kisses me softly,
Ignoring entities who dread the unseen calm
Of agnostic mountain journeys
Because above them galaxies wheel,
Awesome, leaving memory fallen
Into a continuous communication
That feels like punishment.

Do I hate that kind of talk
Because it stinks of fear
Or because I cannot answer
For the night's crazy pinwheel ambassador
When I am exhausted

Or when old wounds flare
In anxious feeling?
Perhaps I was not there
And do not really know.

But I do know
That in this garden of answers,
I will not be attacked
And cannot be captured.
So I seduce or otherwise
Coerce the question—
Charmingly, as a meadowlark,
Raging, as the tiger,
Or eagerly, as the child
Who whispers, "Please do,"
When the spirits of this place
Offer to speak.

The Subject of the Object,
the Object of the Subject

In the Beginning was a contradiction:
The subject/object dichotomy
That seems an inescapable condition
Ingrained in our science, our language,
Our way of perceiving the relationship
Between consciousness and reality.
Some claim the superiority
Of the subject over object,
Make it a political question
And a deliberate power grab
That sows unintentional confusion:
We've all had object lessons;
What about subject lessons?

But if there is no one but subjects,
What of all those other people in the world?
Ask the amorous subject and beloved object
If the subject is superior to the object,
If the object is only derived.
Ask them if subject and object
Are nothing more than creations of mind.
Discuss the relationship between

The real and the illusory; question
The determinative, possessive, and intentional.
Remember the transitive and indirect.
Then remember the circle
When you must decide
Whether the person in the portrait
Is a subject or an object,
Neither subject nor object,
Or both and beyond both.

Meditation on a Forest Path

1

Take the footbridge
And follow the path
Deep into the forest.
The secret path.
The sacred path.
Obvious, inviting,
Marked without signs.

Sometimes the path is paved with rock slabs,
Concrete discovery around each bend.
Sometimes it spans desolate mountain reaches
Raised like dreams of harsh weather,
Where the dawn first shines.
Sometimes it creeps through mossy precincts
Dripping green mystery,
Swallowing shadowy sound,
Echoing primordial seasons
And oracular transformation.

2

This path of unknown antiquity,
Shows the footprints
Of the many who have gone before.
Why do I follow in their wake?
Do I think I can escape the muck
In which their footprints are impressed?
Do I think I can pass without leaving a mark?
Do I think I can find a way out of this forest?
Maybe it would be better
To seek a branch off the beaten path—
Some hidden way deeper into the forest beyond.
But you easily can become lost
Though you head directly toward an objective.
Sometimes the snaky way
Is the shortest.
Sometimes the path up the mountain
Leads to the valley.
Sometimes the divided path
Is the way together.
Sometimes the smallest root that trips
Is a teacher of wisdom.

3

A sylvan glade gives a chance
To rest, to touch the dirt,
To smell musky leaf mold,
To taste the nut that falls
And the berry pending,
To watch the play of dappled light,
To hear bird cries,
And to remember Now.
The trees, solitary yet interwoven,
Solemn in their age, joyful in the transient wind,
Are reminders that this is a forest beyond lyrics
And that peaceful glades can be traps
As well as havens.

4

This is not the forest of infinite wisdom
Or deepest sorrow, love, or confusion.
It is not the forest of violence or redemption.
It is the forest of darkness and light.
Perhaps it is a realm of the Druid network,
Though I have found no gray house in the woods,
And if there are fairies or elves,
I have not seen them.

I see only the effects of time,
Fire, wind, pestilence,
And human dreams
Come to good, ill, or naught.
Even the ancient forest succumbs
To the destruction of the ages.
Does it matter to know,
When there can be no remembering?

5

As I walk, I must not forget
To admire the beauty around me.
Each space between the trees
Invites a new path.
Which should I take?
Where will it lead?
But as I follow the twisted and tangled way
Barely visible through the terrain of trees,
A sense comes that there is only one way to go
Though other paths branch
And different destinations
Tantalize in glimpses.
Perhaps it is enough to trace the network,
For all ways are lost in the forest.
All lost.

6

In the forest's shadows,
In moments of solitude,
It seems as if this forgotten path,
Beaten hard at the dawn of time by sauropod
And trailing out beneath a dying sun,
Leads beyond discovery
Because its pathfinders
Are not just pioneers or pilgrims,
But creators giving form to void.

Age and Recompense

1

In an age of darkness dawning,
We seek the door of recompense,
Phantom, intractable,
Invaluable in its exploration,
Ongoing in its regulation,
Fabled in its promise.
But our notion of recompense
Has a barbarian flavor.
Blood is usually involved,
And the enactment of deeds
That require further recompense.
The local cemetery is filled
With innocence, affection, and gratitude,
Headstones bestowing the rebuke
Of an age awestruck,
Devoid of myth,
Seeking the one light
That will forever elude it.

2

Recompense can only embellish loss,
Provide an avenue of complaint,
And advance the symptoms
Of disease and dissolution
In proportion to its performance.
Give me the soothsayer's unknowable truth,
But spare me the lies of recompense
As old age comes to wear me to oblivion.
I wish no relationship with it.
I deny it has knowledge worth knowing.
I say it is a mark of self-delusion
And deeds undone
And an abode that never was a home
And where no one ever visits.
It is a relationship
Between luck and lies
And gifts of death.
Give me not recompense
But physical phenomena.
They have no grace,
Their rewards are not magnificent,
Their consequences are often withheld,
Their secrets are as well guarded
As patience and acts of mercy,

But they do not dwell in the vengeance
Of pious regimes
That make recreation
Of destruction, pain, and death.
Those who cannot transform
Their own blood
Will be surrounded by blood
And propagate a hateful age.

3

Cardboard crowds
Grasping at the surfaces of things
Do not know that an entire fortune
Is neither recompense nor sufficient buffer
For the chill poverty of this forsaken age
Of rote morals that cannot admit
The criminal and damning involvement
Of each and every one of us.
Call it the Kingdom of Heaven
Or the House of Allah or Nirvana,
But the notion exists within the human mind:
A place perfectly corrupt with selfish intent.
Religion places us outside the all-encompassing,
Without the all-encompassing,

Gives permission to sin through the promise
Of absolution by prayer and fealty.
How cheap and foolish:
Attempting to appease the unappeasable,
To persuade the unpersuadable,
To bargain and beg
For the elimination of a past
That has made you what you are
And all that you can be.

So do not detain me in the establishment
Of your Endless Age to Come.
I wish only to go on,
Away from your catacombs
And martyrs and centuries
Of self-deluded interpretation
Of texts you simply Believe in.
The afterlife is this life,
And until you understand that,
You will be forever doomed
To this purgatory of recompense.
I prefer science's oblivion.

4

I know that amazing beauty makes no sense
To a concrete thinker.
I know that the age-old struggle
Of the mystery of the human heart
Is lost to the minds of tyrants,
The artificers of sickness,
The thieves who steal our shadows.
But I long for something more than
A ritual of shame and chastising lash,
Something more than hidden snares of hatred
And quagmires of righteous blood,
The stumbling blocks of useless atrocities,
The miseries of apprehension,
The very notion of compensation
That leaves us without recourse or notification.

5

After this age's convulsions, storms, and heat,
What is just recompense?
The good life?
The peak of performance?
Continued growth?
A golden age?

We have passed from an age
Of myth and fable—
Where heroes strode a world
Fraught with hidden meaning,
Seeking mystery and transformation—
To an age of suspense, revenge, and feud,
Whose heroes are without prophecies
Or well-directed valor.
And though they may mouth
The dispensations of grace,
They hunger only to kill and eat.

In a practical age like ours,
Where only the literal and the surface count
And we might not even own our own DNA,
We shall not want
For an instant definition
Or for a rifle.
But where is luck?
Where is the stuff of wizards
In this unwholesome, penurious prison
Where debts are paid with bones
And the only recompense for a youth
Wasted by the beggary of this age
Is a demand for vengeance?
Where are the just desserts

That are no empty paeans of victory?
In this age, blind to itself
And plundering through fields of the dead,
We have become the travel agents,
Ticket takers, baggage handlers,
And passengers to catastrophe.

6

What reward, prize, or payment
Can make up for the evils of a world
Where no thread of justice, moderation, or faith
Or some other virtue of steadfastness
Can vanquish obsessions
Little changed since the Stone Age?
We are struck with ingratitude,
Forced onto the scrap heap of hope,
Dealing with questions of amount,
Wracked with notions and tyrannies
That contradict our own ideals
And affirm the landscape of barbaric outrage
Across which we wander,
Searching vainly for the best of what we have done
And consoling ourselves
With memories of the taste of summer.

When the Age of Upheaval is past,
How shall we move forward?
Will we cease to bathe in nostalgia
And taste the summer, not memories?
It is not gone.
It is here in our breasts.
It is the message we hear with closed ears,
Borne by a stealthy messenger
Come on feet of brass,
Eyes aflame with sight
That pierces deeper than any surface.

7

Having reached the proper age,
Having found no peace and taken no spoils,
Having too long provoked the struggle
Of luck and practical usefulness,
I feel like an unwelcome guest forcibly removed
Into a bad age for wanderers.
A long defeat creates orphans
And leaves them groveling among the shards
Of history, culture, and civilization

For some jewel in the rough
That is but small recompense
For enduring futile obstruction.

Grasping vainly for memories
Of affection, gratitude, and valor,
We have died without remembering
That community is composed
Of that which we cannot measure,
For which we keep no record but our hearts.

Work and Aching Denial

There are so many hard surfaces
Where people live and work,
And folk wisdom is filled with ghosts
Who hunger to be normal
Instead of angular in a smooth place,
Ghosts who know but one chance in infinity
Of finding a good haunt,
Ghosts, isolated, realizing they hear
The distant cracking of the whip,
Ghosts whose spasms have stopped.

Thus I find myself a reflective practitioner
In a mist of forgetfulness and denial,
Caught in my daydream
Of creatures aching for heroic leaders.
Here is how it works:
Signs and symptoms,
Causes of complaints,
The monstrous denial of our true nature,
The slyly anonymous pitchfork mind.

And then it's over before it's even begun.

Boundary Survey

1

To understand tectonic plate motions,
You must realize that all
The action is at the edges—
In boundary currents,
In velocities and divergence,
In type, composition, and implication,
Verified and endorsed by a survey of details.
Take a voyage to the region
Where magnetic anomalies
Reverse polarities
Whether you like it or not.

It is impossible to delineate boundaries
When all is shifting,
When mid-oceanic ridges
Spill out new land, spitting and steaming,
And send it creeping toward
Terrain we once thought timeless,
Leaving us helpless to do more
Than survey parameters

That are never more than eddies
Swirling but a moment in time
Then vanishing for eternity
Beneath the subduction zones
Of history and the limits of human memory.

2

If we believe in anything,
It is in discontinuity and expendability,
In circulation and interaction,
And a future like an enormous room
Filled with marred antique furniture
That simulates the asymmetries
And distributed deformation
Of the dense, rigid nature of collision.

So send us charts
Of the human dimension
Made with low-altitude surveys
And line-of-sight readings
Taken by those who have been to and returned
From zones that straddle correlation and velocity.
Let us study the occurrence and structure

Of upwelling, the role of meltwater,
The observations of temperature fronts
With surrounding oceanic waters.
The skewness of temperature
And interactions of turbulent transfer
Serve as references for sensitivity tests
That characterize adopted anomalies.
Coherent flow patterns
Require integration of terrain
With external forces,
But if you perceive just a suggestion
Of a serpentine presence
Along almost any boundary,
Pretend it's only subsurface chill.

3

It requires no survey to know that fire
Coincides with locations of divergence,
That plumes of hot mantle bloom from the core.
There is no stability in these crushing zones
Where mineral gneissis
Accumulates and deforms,
Where density and contrast characterize

The dynamics of identification.
A survey only determines the zone boundary
Through which we are passing,
Defines the morphology
Of the structures of our turbulent constraints.

The Oracle's Box

The True If Tenuous Elasticity of Clouds

In the domain of those who fly,
Abstract, unsupported,
Impossible to select
Or to remove all trace of,
How does one attach
To topography that may expand
To any shape or size?

In fleets that browse over the landscape
And reroute at the slightest request
Or prodding of frequent error,
Unable to perform query,
Cheat the latest opportunities,
Or choose the right image,
Clouds deliver on the promise
Of building entire concepts
For each discovery process.

Cloud Washing at Its Best

The Transparent Oracle is lovely.
It lives in a glass box because
Of its uncanny accuracy,
Flawless image, keen memory,
Moments of great triumph,
And secrets that draw the jealousy
Of the vast Milky Way.
Why do experts on the oracle
Never seem to consider
That it is truly oracular?
Because they cannot see it,
Some do not believe
That it even exists.

The oracle was unveiled
During a journey
Full of torment, of error,
Of significant weather—
Ancient realms allowed to speak
In the next riddle:
We know what you seek,
Even if you are unsure yourself.

Cloud Mechanics

Imagine yourself presented with this box.
A glass box.
A system divine.
Introduced to the world's first and only,
Only if you can reveal
Its most sensitive secrets.
Tools you will be using:
Stone, hammer, crowbar, anvil.

Is there really an oracle in that box:
Jack's wiser sibling popping out,
Generating mystifying responses
To the social community
Taking place in the world of forms?

Once I thought of taking a deeper look
Inside to discover the key
To a fiendishly unbreakable alchemical code
The speaking of which instantly
Sounds the true name of any object
And the true meaning of any heart.
But I did not have the vision
Required to take that deeper look.

The Strategy of Clouds

Unable to avoid caution—
The gut-level process of analysis—
It is time to think inside the box,
Time to disconnect the dots
That define the discongruity
Of the automated and disciplined,
Time to rally to the beat
Of the wild arena:
Without demand,
Without predictive purposes,
Without force.

When other people make your constraints,
Your values, your destination and purpose,
The physical limits of memory
Are most likely in error.
The path of security does not allow
Any man to get away with making bets
No man dare make.

Putting a Cloud in a Box

To see the unseen is truly a miracle.
Write down a name for it
More stunning than letters can spell.
But nothing is more complex than retrieving.
This morning announced
A complete refresh of the sun,
And in its light, the box appears empty.
After all, the oracle does not speak
Unless it wants to,
And clouds are not in a box,
And they never will be in a box.

The Tissue of Sight

Foresight

There is no substitute
For the tissue of human sight.
It is not extracted, like Kleenex,
From a convenient floral dispenser.
Used, it ultimately becomes
The parameter of the awesome;
Misused, it separates
From its sense of absolute doubt,
Blinds before the brain
Clouds the ability to see.

In Search of Sight

The opaque surface of culture
Does not allow light to effectively
Enter the central nervous system.
While scientists seek to unlock
The mystery of identity
And the schema of hope,
Touch, taste, hearing, smell, and sight

Are replaced by one's own cells
In a regeneration shaped
Within the human skull.

Sight Unseen

History conceals expression of a single thought,
Illustrates that where the damaged and scarred
Are confused with the cloudy and diseased,
We settle for something
That behaves almost as if human.

Out of Sight

Language goes beyond sight,
Even beyond sound,
But it is difficult to harness
The meanings of words
To the cart of intention.
Don't despair:
There is no deadline,
And the quilt of words you sew
Is never finished.

Candied Apple Agony

1

Candied apples:
Frankly and unflinchingly sexual—
A hard core sales pitch
On the midway of life.
And, oh agony, oh Bible man,
A people's history—
Candid in its cadence and record,
Fierce beyond the chance of cannon,
Beyond mouths surpassed,
Beyond years of war and hysteria,
Beyond the pain of having
And loss.
Beyond care.

2

I warn you:
The rotten apple is reserved for His age.
If you want a real definition of agony,
Do not look to the stations
Of Calvary's cross.

Watch those they told
To take a bite of the rotten apple
Become landmarks of national agony
Who do not permit a candid appraisal of agony
And look away from the truth
And fall further into agony.
Though the preacher tossed
The apple of knowledge high
And millions saw it fall,
They did not see gravity.

3

Secreted in primal gardens,
Aphrodite's golden apples hang
Like comprehensive topics
And inspirational categories,
Like the resources of description
Aggressive in appearance,
Straightforward, and vivid in detail.
One is a description of appetites
Cancelled in experience:
Have your mouth open
When they shake the apple tree.

4

Love isn't visual,
And this passionate story about
Joy and the embrace of release
Is a bitter phantom, hidden
Yet responding with combative applause.
Humans' first act of love
Is to vent their agony,
Full-fledged, said alone, said to loss,
Honoring ambiguous, arduous coercion.
No wonder the most painful experiences
Are change and the struggle
To become the menace of transitions
In a powerful and abrupt realm.
But this first act is a secret crush
Gone deceitful and a bit ridiculous.
Can't you imagine the agony of shade
Facing candescent astronomy?
Have your mouth open
When they shake the apple tree.

5

Divine from the falling of the inductive school,
I stammered through a romantic agitation
That was like a debt almost wild with rage.
And for one moment,
In air calmed by encounter,
When her body had robbed
My agony of its destruction,
I slumped, speechless with diffidence,
Tossed by a storm of grief,
And cradling a scientific version
Of the first act to vent its agony,
Full-fledged, alone.

Exhausted by the effort of undertaking form,
I heard, reverberating through my windowpane,
A dream singing on an apple bough—
A dream now lost in whispers
Of a silent response
Whose tongue is as quick
As the serpent of the accounts of sin.

6

The way the neck turns, the head must follow,
And you, sermon, are my favorite child—
The apple of my eye—
Though you sit in shadows.
I don't know if you saw a horizon,
Renegade and dark,
But I cannot stop what fate means
Or keep from venting my spleen,
Or cavorting upon the questions,
Or insisting on touching
And enduring knowing,
Though I cannot touch what agony aged.
I cannot touch that child in the shadows,
Pure as a hypocrite,
Large as muttering,
Addressing possible providence.
I can find only opinions reminiscent
Of the voices a ship collects in its sails
As it plies familiar routes,
Of a mist in the morning,
Of remarks regarding another sighting
Of the rocks of reconciliation,
Where the cry of capture
Is the only testament.

7

That familiar agony, that agony of all,
Is why posed and candid photographs
Look so different.
It becomes a bridge
To what we need to know,
To the qualifications necessary
To respect another and possibly be another.
So I continue moving toward that feast of apples
And try to be very candid and honest,
But first I must endure the agony of you who sing.

8

I cannot entirely fathom what you offer me
Except the knowledge
That Omphalos yet attends the dance.
But the song of reason still haunts
The branches of the apple tree
Whose fruit is as sweet
As the agitation of cancellation,
As silky as smoky blossoms,
Always startling, often wry.

The frustration and effort were enough
To turn me on a sharp accent.
Though grateful for the challenging questions
And penetrating insights,
I gathered in my tambourine
Only the coin of foolish universal applause.
Expression becomes so purgatorial
That it is impossible to venture
Through all that great agony
To express virtues from a footing of sand
Except to confess that love
Lacks nothing in its moments of transaction
With a foolish world.

9

Our first reaction was negative:
A position needlessly detained
In a domain preaching expression.
We were so simple, so grave.
I trust you will be candid enough to believe
That I remember the agony, the lessons—
Solemnly, earnestly, reverently, faithfully.

Counsel's chastised attentiveness,
Conservation's betrayal,
Agony's accusing conviction
Are the marks that conquer me,
That confirm the laws,
That value misunderstanding.
But let there be no misunderstanding:
Though I've never caught the golden apples,
I cannot crush my candied apple
And calamitously squander and curtail surprise.

10

Ah, impulsively,
You are nervously identifying,
Personally intensifying the impact,
Empathizing with their agony
In the middle of the night.
Forget it.
It will only bring sleeplessness.
It is no joke that humor heals.
When people laugh, apple-cheeked,
The agony fades down the midway.
Laughs and fades.

Dispensation of the Reckless

The storms of ruthless dispensation
And the strategic hubris of a pastime paradise
Have struck my mind numb
With an image of shadows kneeling in prayer.
Why does any belief deserve dispensation
For stunningly fierce hatred of good,
For forfeited truth, for compliant madness,
For a treacherous and reckless conceit
Swollen into a rootless representation
Of wisdom strapped and shackled by a past
That has no history?

The Trial of Music

Audition Anxiety

Facing charges of breaching laws
Prescribing automatic design for a suitable period.
Witnesses subpoenaed to testify.
Pleas bargained like items at a bazaar.
"I deserve a fair trial like every American."

The Circus Begins

The importance of this trial is unparalleled.
The prisoner who stands before you
Was caught red-handed improvising.
Read his confession yourself:
"Our music may change your life
Or that of someone you know."

Allegro

The bloody evidence:
A score of dark and sensual ambience.
The controversial information:

The mythology was overshadowing the music
With tales of rise, pleasures, and downfall.

Key witnesses take the stand:
The fan,
The groupie,
The warm-up band,
The music critic,
The photographer.
Guitar riffs and melodic twilight.

The prosecution paints the Big Picture:
"The following opinions about music
Are based on reports of scientific studies."
The defense picks at faulty technique:
"If you examine music theory
From scales through secondary dominants,
You will see the witness is not qualified
To testify about the odds
Of a plane crash survivor becoming a musician."

A controlled witness takes the stand:
"No one ever really asked about their music."
And one not so controlled:
"I never place myself in so vulnerable a position."

Every trial is a story of human complexity
In which the verdict does not rely on truth
But on who tells the best tale,
And justice is improvised
By those who were not there.
"We believe the jury will find that music is worthy.
A new sort of trial should be held.
And remember, music makes you smarter!"

Savage Swings in the Jury Room

Deliberation involving scales.
Piracy.
Mixing.
Playing notes that shouldn't be played.
Some music gets better with repeated listening,
Some only fades,
Lame,
Cranky,
Homogenous.

The Verdict

Intuitive, improvised.
Equipped with an incredible array of functions.

Adapted to the needs of everyone.
Meant for live consumption.
Maps onto your evolutionary path of light
And activates your DNA.
Enhances your meditations.
Will you comprehend the give-and-take?

The Sentence

Be careful what you wish for:
It is difficult to choose the right fate
When you can't submit your requirements,
When you participate in the fading of magnitude,
When you live in territory explored by scuffles,
When you are disillusioned
With randomized purpose,
When ingenuity emerges stagnant
And no category fits.

Punishment Phase

In due submission, bend and sway.

Considering Other Steps

0

We are here.
All other areas are open,
And achieving full potential
Will require other steps.

1

Stretch vision,
Reasoning as one would teach
About objects worth considering
And the formalism of topics
And ways to improve dialogue,
With the right notes pacing
The steps of the dance.
But can we be satisfied
With the incremental vision
Received as a result?
Are structure and organization
Esoteric signposts on the path
To a challenging and provocative future
Or a means of prohibition and prevention?

2

Can small, near destinations
Sustain our eternal dialogue?
Small steps have the catastrophic potential of large
In the architecture of feverish memory
Where the chimes of clocks
Stride into the future ahead of us,
Numbering the impositions of death
And the final accounts of prophecies.

Consider what remains
After the removal of contingency
And the arrangement of sources:
The confidence of fear,
The arguments of impulse,
The distance of touch,
And the symptoms of rehabilitation.
When will we be capable of synthesis?
When will we recognize copies of surprise?
What will be the severity of the problem,
The risks of consistency,
The suggestions of innovation,
The merits of treasure?

3

No stride of time, large or small,
Can sidestep criteria contained
In manifestos' recommendations
When human history
Does not consider serenity.

Armed with the causes of prevention,
We must turn from the worst possible conclusions
To unsubstantiated folklore and rumor
And the ubiquitous interactions of archetypes.
There are three thousand steps to heaven,
But before we proceed,
Affirmation seems the appropriate, the consistent,
The significant, and the difficult decision:
No more stolen lives!

4

We must make distortion a thing of the past.
We must take away with one hand
And take more with the other.
We must designate experiential starting points
But not neglect the waiting times
Between the spaces of involvement.

Within our collective heart,
Beating in cadence anonymous,
Vague, conditional, bounded, yet resilient,
Our dispositions, undertakings, and goals
Are challenges of place and circumstance.

5

Time's necessary effect,
Simultaneous, consuming, contentious,
Uses techniques that don't make sense.
Consider the number of futility.
It is infinite.
Consider the building of endeavor.
It is eternal.
Consider deviations from models.
They are no less circumstantial
Than the evidence of standards.
Now consider unconfirmed
Rumors about approximation
And the occupants of otherwise.

What do we consider simplicity and multiplicity?
Why do multiple iterations become obligations?
How can idea be a flexible acquisition?

When is reflection an alternative for prevention?
Where is the issue of motivation?
Who might prevent us from considering
Risk just another perspective,
Another resource, another motivation?

6

Certainty is an ultimatum
That abhors inconveniences
And plots the future like a chess player
But does not address the wounds of capacity
Or designs hidden from control.
But there are certainties:
The day is illuminated by the sun.
Persons affect each other through action.
Just as destinations require steps,
Steps require destinations.
There are no destinations.
There are steps.

7

There seems no choice but to
Reevaluate, verify, elaborate,
Supplement, analyze, investigate,
And contribute energy.
These are the modes corresponding
To the overall courses of action and reaction.
These are the actualizations of incremental works.
These are the steps.
But if we are not to become stuck,
Like an old dog who can't climb the stairs,
We must reconsider a thousand times more
The gestalt of the fog that leaves the dew.
We must take the measure of the immeasurable
And tread the spaces between the steps.

Enhancement of the Recommended

When life gets you down,
Try an enhancement of the recommended.
It has been used successfully
With no adverse side effects,
Is fully approved,
Will enable you to automatically answer.
Includes measures to offset past sedimentation.
The results are amazing!

Choose one or more of the following:
Strategy
Action
Responsibility
Immunity
Priority
Preparation
Emphasis
Availability.

If you are overcorrected,
If you experience a fluctuation,
Reject options that fail to beautify the view.

An evaluation includes:
Specific techniques for development,
Preliminary connection to various surfaces,
Prioritized listing of concept comparisons,
And restoration for full development.*

Bringing together the functions
And building on the achievements of the agencies,
The method is memory-intensive,
Cognitive in focus, durable in agreement,
Tailored to the process of analyzed results.
It negotiates assessments of alternate capacities,
Explores objectives of criteria,
Implements a totally changed understanding,
Provides information about roses.**

But the situation is not as black and white
As high-intensity exposures
Would have us believe.
Considerations are ambient,
Clarifications compensate,
Motivation composes activity,
Determination emphasizes change.
In a future of certainty and safety,
There is no augmentation
That has not been modified

To resemble Ouroboros.
If we could avoid certainty and safety,
We would be like aircraft operating
Below minimum altitudes,
Discovering new details.

* Comprehensive and final actions are not provided.
** Always be aware.

Monastic Distortion Ceremony

In a copy of tradition,
Everything was set:
The authorities,
The crowds,
The rite,
The new liturgy
Of a narrow subjectivism
Bleeding mediocrity and distortion
From wounds deep
In time spent in this world.
But even the worst evil
And error in this world
Have no power over
Fire-and-brimstone Buddhism
Or angelic rage
Because the precise wording
Of any ceremony
Is a denial of reality.

What should flow through the instrument
Without distortion, without shadow?
Reason seems inevitable,
But it is a no less caustic ceremony
That leaves a brutal slab of red

And the begetting of monsters
As the price for comprehensibility
And for learning that reason,
Being relative in time and space,
Distorts reality no less than madness.

How can we live without the unknown before us?
Imagination and memory eclipse identity,
Warp like a flaw in a cheap looking-glass,
And become entry points of an unholy resonance
In which the distractions of innocence
Are drowned in pious temperatures.
Success will take desperate remedies
And an ironic assumption
Of the essence of meaning condemned to silence
Where high peaks meet pure ether.

Encyclopedia of Solar Flares

1

Solar flares—
Hot, towering, highly energetic,
Intricately licking icy emptiness,
Lashing out at fantastic speeds,
And spitting enormous quantities
Of matter and energy into the void.
Their encyclopedia is exhaustive,
Liberally illustrated with stunning photos
And filled with examples
As transient as a match flame,
As indispensably significant
As eruptions of our own hearts.

The foreword contains warning signs
Charred and buffeted by solar winds:
Radiation hazard.
Spacecraft beware.
Polar aircraft beware.
Power grids beware.
Computers beware.
Even within our own planetary sphere,

We are vulnerable
And never know when
We might be burned to a cinder.

2

It is very educational, this catalog
Of temperature and spectrum,
Of geomagnetic storms and plasma clouds
And the seeming antithesis that flares
Are associated with sunspots' darkness.
We learn of flares' origins
In the sun's chromosphere,
That their rage in the corona
Beats out the solar wind,
That the wind washes the planets
And distorts their atmospheres
And magnetic fields.
We read terms such as facula,
Quiescent prominences,
Eruptive prominences.
We learn that coronal mass ejections
Are released once or twice a decade,
Like the pent-up hatred of petty tyrants.
But none of this matters

When we are touched and flush.
Aren't the auroras brilliantly beautiful
When flares scorch our atmosphere?

3

Although we are all too human,
We are required to ride these solar flares,
Whose high speeds and acute trajectories
Make this dangerous sport, indeed.
So we research the various special mechanisms
Of magnetic induction and radioisotopes,
We trap solar wind samples
In high-resolution magnetographs
To invoke revelations of background information
And randomly assign surface environments.
We witness the severe genesis of failed eruptions
That become enormous whirling storms
Wrinkling the skin of the sun.

What is the definitive event?
What is the primary phenomenon?
What is the regular observation?
What is the reference to discovery?
Or are there only acceleration

And kinetics
And synthesis
And examination?
Perhaps flares are complete without us;
Perhaps only with us.
Perhaps we are merely collateral damage
Or secret, surprised canaries of prediction
Exposed to a full range of phenomena.
If we could but refract to show our different layers,
Perhaps we might learn
That the most frequently observed events
Are sudden, localized, transient increases
In brightness associated with periods
Of intense activity and hazard.

But all we hear now is the cry of science
Citing the basics of perturbation and disruption.
We shall need only:
Facts.
Demonstrations.
Order.
Warning signs.
Sunscreen.

Fact: The sun rings like a bell.
Can you hear it ring?

4

Seen at the raw edge of an occluded solar disk,
Solar winds are perpetual streams of information
In which composition and power do not reflect
And are not restricted to the visible.
In a background that varies with specific activity,
The profound impact of energetic outbursts
Appear over time and at different wavelengths.
Such data might provide information
On how minute variations in the sun
Affect changes in our weather,
But because there is no strict pattern,
The propagation of thresholds
Propelled by forces of interactions
Cannot be predicted.
With no immediately identifiable manifestation,
Can there be a verifiable result?

Rather than crowd thousands of years
Into observations that trace regions
Of perturbation and diffraction,
Observe adventures of surprise.
Go and witness for yourself
The solar wind lifting off from the sun.
Watch the synthesis of reclamation and transition.

Heed potential warnings, old and new.
Check the effects of instability and acceleration,
Of a skillful and compelling argument
For stimulated and heightened processes.
Notice that scales change with flares' brightness.
Notice that observations usually cover the similar.
Notice the details of history and prophecy.
Realize that information is not a curious nuisance
And that the largest sunspot is the source
Of numerous flares and coronal mass ejections.
Learn that sunspots are unexplained, unfathomed.

5

Do you see only what the eye sees?
If we had some other sort of vision,
We could gaze with excitement
Into the hearts of solar flares.
Supernovas, neutron stars, and black holes
Might reveal their vaster secrets.
But we are children lost in space
With an umbilical attachment to a monotheism
That cannot peer into the heart
Of a cityscape at night,
With its dusk that never terminates,

With its stony cavities
That solar flares cannot touch,
With its delay of life's current
Ironically called interpretation.

Are we learning that solar flares cause mutations,
Transferable skills, or a bitter, burning end?
We know them only as infectious bombardment,
An irritation that plays havoc with communication.
We cannot yet know how big a problem
They will be for those living on the moon
Or if there is information to be gained
From the received wisdom
Of unvarnished luminosity.

6

Accept that flares, coronal mass ejections,
And other such activities
Follow cycles.
Think of a new propulsion
That goes beyond
The ionosphere's imperfect medium
Of interrupted transmissions.
Dream of the shock

Of a reciprocal organicosmic chromosome.
Feel the wind that stretches connection,
And seek to know who sends these solar flares,
These demonstrations,
These disasters,
These treasures.

Blindman's Bluff

1

In moments of anger,
If we could just
Laugh like children
With no surprises beyond
The face in the mirror
Or familiar signs of a misspent youth,
We would all agree we would not
Change if we could.
In the end, we are just a bluff
Dressed up in fiction
And handpicked for desperation:
Good people always at the hour of death
Taking desperate steps
Through a carnage that reaches out blindly,
Only to find we have,
In our darkness, stumbled.
But sometimes, sometimes,
There is a glimmer of light,
And we can see
Those we stumble upon.

2

The rolling seas of ancient lovers
Seeking dimensions that frame
The background of dreams
Mark the psychological limits of delight.
They are variations on a theme.
They are why we appoint identities,
Reissue arbitrations, and forge a legacy of lies.
They propagate the wave that rides toward shore,
Strikes, and collapses with both hands,
Leaving petals wilting in the sand
Before it retreats into a medium
The shade of ghosts.

3

Like a bad word caught
In a cluster of good names,
Like a wretched tragedy,
Like the black storm
Of silent mad laughter in the dark,
Our curious martial history
Avoids suspicion
In its perfectly contented reverie.

We clap our hands at its performance
Or pretend we just don't feel rain
At the crossroads of ill-advised passion
As we wait for a green light
That never comes.

We live in an age of discovery,
Yet it is forbidden to speak of progress
Outside of the dialect of metaphor or symbolism.
In self-preservation, we simply depart
From the vainglorious demands of cannibals
Who would see the seeker encompassed
By the art of self-consumption.

4

Stranded in transgression,
We observe the forms of disintegration.
If we were to touch, in our darkness,
The metaphysics of abandonment,
We might feel enthusiasm at its ideals,
Be satisfied in a space both domestic and foreign,
Feel the enthusiasm of wonder
Joined with ignorance
Instead of the bite of cynicism
Joined with old games of truth.

There is no justice,
Only an exhaustion that knows
There is no comfort in winning
And that we are sworn to secrecy
About the things we do.

5

Of what good is echolocation
In the blind alleys of an invisible universe?
There is no acoustic evidence of illusion,
Nor can we devise imagery that depicts objects
Beyond their shadows,
Beyond a dream made of fragrance
And a moment of grace.
I thought I built such a dream
With my own conscience
And devotion to that ancient strain
Between mystery and disbelief—
Then it was gone,
Leaving mere shapes of history
And a pocketful of keys whose locks
Have long since vanished.

Traveling the Western Trail

1

Let us venture along the Western Trail.
This is no tame trail of the merely curious:
No Allegheny or Mohawk or Wilderness.
This is the real thing: the physical diary
Of the desperate and dissatisfied
Etched across the terrain of history,
Blazed through the American ethos,
Blazing in our hearts.
It ventures across seemingly endless expanses
Of prairie, plain, and desert,
Over mountains and the spine of a continent,
Past the outposts and forts of dangerous lands
Peopled with the anger of trespass.
This is the scenery of our heritage,
Of future national park and monument,
Though vegetation now covers the old dirt tracks.

2

Men, women, and children alike
Caught Western fever—
More than half a million pulled up stakes
And abandoned familiar surroundings
For the dust of trails that faced the western winds,
For the trails of hope that chased the sun,
For the trails that promised rest for the weary feet
Of the generations that followed their footsteps.
Let us remember the names:
Daniel Boone's Trail,
The Lewis and Clark Trail,
The Bridger Trail,
The Old Spanish Trail,
Fosston's Trail,
The Santa Fe Trail,
Bryant's Trail,
The Butterfield Trail,
The Old Pecos Trail,
The Mormon Trail,
The Bozeman Trail,
The Oregon Trail,
The Pacific Northwest Trail,
The Chihuahua Trail,
The Rubicon Trail,
The California Trail.
We forget the Trail of Tears.

3

Think of the pioneers, so hungry for a new dawn
That they risked their remaining days.
Think of the hard, weary miles
Of blistering heat, rain, snow, starvation, bad water.
Think of the graves—
One in ten died on their Pacific journey.
Then think of their wagons traveling together,
Their stamina, their purpose
That lets no feature of terrain, no hazard,
Stand in the way.
There were no maps,
Just trust in the tracks
Of those who'd gone before.

4

Trailblazers!
Moving, always moving
And fighting and overrunning
Until they thought the trail was safe
For the life of a new nation burgeoning
Beneath the loam of hardship and excitement.
They believed in an end to the wilderness.

They thought there were western destinations
And a home at the edge of the horizon.
Their wagons traveled together, always together.

5

What was that river?
That valley?
That mountain?
Do they have names?
The travelers could not pause to name them.
Only the generations that followed
Could name the features and know them all.
And when the American frontier
Finally found its Pacific barrier,
When the pioneer diaries and letters
Finally gave way to newspapers
And telegraph office
And digital realms,
What was the truth about traveling west?
Can we name its most important legacy?
It is our pilgrimage along the trail of memories
Our forebears left traced on the landscape.
What genre is more beloved of America

Than the Western?
What figure more iconic
Than the cowboy?
What conflict more anticipated
Than the high-noon shoot-out?
What conveyance more famed
Than the covered wagon?
What place more entrenched
Than the cavalry outpost or frontier town?
What stop more poignant
Than the trailside grave?
Just watch the vacationers
Mimic movement over old ground:
Minivans replacing covered wagons,
Motels replacing outposts,
Park rangers replacing cavalry riders.
The shoot-outs are on the streets back home.

6

Somewhere along the trail,
In one of those roadside graves,
Is the triumph of a tragedy
That echoes through time and culture.
There we buried the knowledge

That what we find at the end of the trail
Is the boundary of a new wilderness
And the beginning of an even longer trail.
There we buried the yearning for a quest
That is not marked on ordinary maps
But only in our hearts—
A trail with no terminus, only perspectives.

The Empty Quarter

I seek the empty quarter, discover many,
And any might do:
Mysterious, vast, cruel, hostile, shifting,
Trackless as far as the eye can see.

There is the Rub al-Khali in Arabia,
Where Bedouin and djinn roam
Over the ruins of ancient cities
Succumbed to the drifts of time.

There is the Black Rock Desert in Nevada,
Where mirages shimmer dreams of ancient seas,
And the playa is the place
Of speed records and devotees of burning men.

There is one called Paraguay,
Where the jungle remains unknown
Except to the dangerous people born there
And war criminals' barren madness.

There is one in the ocean west of South America,
Where so few roam
That even UFO sightings
Are washed away by the waves.

There is one in southwest Tasmania,
Where bog holes clutch like a jealous lover,
Whose heart is sucked dry by new development
With a greedier grasp.

There is one in Scotland,
Where island mountains rising above
A tartan of lochs and overgrown roads mask
Villages abandoned to a superb sense of space.

There is the Great Bend Sand Prairie in Kansas,
Where thin skins of grass lie over the dunes,
And only a small change in climate could give life
To a little Rub al-Khali right in America's heartland.

There is one in space,
Where the flares of ancient nebulae
Are but flickers in infinity
And infinity is swallowed by eternity.

There are many others:
Empty pockets,
Empty porches,
Empty words,
Empty roads,
Empty rooms.
There is the new moon
And the old one.
There are digital deserts.
There are changing positions and big myths.
There are conspiracy, collaboration, complicity.
All are mysterious, vast, cruel, hostile, shifting,
Trackless as far as the eye can see.

We are enchanted by the abodes of emptiness
And compelled to demarcate their boundaries
And cross them and catalogue and fill them
And finally contain the deadly black hold
They have on our imaginations.
But no explorer, cartographer, or diplomat,
No scientist, psychologist, or missionary
Has successfully defined the borders
Of the one empty quarter that matters most:
The one deep in the human heart.

Coda

1

I am absolutely convinced
That the universe does all the work,
That all of creation
Is a part of God's glorious being,
But I will not be perplexed by fiery halos
Or blown by the ferocious
Yet careless breath of implausibility.
Purists will be annoyed by
Reification
Falsification,
Elaboration,
Exaggeration.
And I, for their sake,
But also because distortion
Of the essence of life
Can leave so durable an impression
That it gives lie
To any learned and lucid survey of thought.

2

People aren't tokens;
They leave imprints on each other.
There is no escape from completeness
And its elementary archetype:
A rabid outbreak that just says yes
Without asking for verification
Of the number of the phases of grief.
But denial is a trait buried deep
Within our genetic being,
And we will not give ourselves opportunity
To integrate our humanity
Before we trample the Earth
And poison our own dens.

3

Memory's reckless lucidity
Is a sickness as old as insights
That have staled into technique,
Technique that has staled into complacency.
This should be a time of planting seeds—
That paradox of optimism without resolution—
Not a darkness that unravels ages,
Not a mordant outlook

That forges a global mystery of conjecture
Charted only by maps without terrains
Pulled from deep in the basement,
Showing shy smiles of bad teeth,
Betraying the embarrassed shoulders
Of deep and self-aware lack of sophistication.
To simplify, place the idea of revenge
In the cramped and miserable prison cell
Memory built to hold uncontainable
Hope, love, and responsibility.

4

You have heard of people whose battles
Are won or lost on the basis of a single dance.
It is a dance danced to a song once sung.
It is a dance along paths that intersect
In mutual concourse and rhythm.
It is a dance through air prepared and ruled
By a jurisdiction beyond sound.
It is a dance that moves even the lifeless.
It is the dance of the future.
The future does not dance madly backward
Nor dive to the depths
To wait until the storm passes.
It is the storm, and it never passes.

So when the charlatan voices of unreason unleash
Judgments based on arguments
Dangerously close to circular,
They should be careful what they wish for.
The realities of freedom and independence
Might walk the halls of an asylum
Whose atmosphere reeks of trial and error,
But better to endure unspeakable torment
While trying to access the heart of a faerie oracle
To learn the legends of the seasons
Than to deny the changes of the year.

5

On the same morning,
Three signs arrived from different continents:
There wouldn't be reason, but there might be rhyme;
There would be no danger, but there might be thrills;
There would be observance honed through time.
So, in the absence of absence,
Still, heart. Quiet.

Phosphene Publishing Company publishes books and DVDs related to literature, drama, history, Texana, film, the paranormal, spirituality, and the martial arts.

For other great titles, visit
phosphenepublishing.com